CUSTOM

THE PEAK

&

DERBYSHIRE

BY

JOHN N. MERRILL

Best wishes,

John N. Merrill

Maps and photographs by John N. Merrill.

a J.N.M. PUBLICATION

1988

a J.N.M. PUBLICATION

JNM PUBLICATIONS,
WINSTER,
MATLOCK,
DERBYSHIRE.
DE4 2DQ

Conceived, edited, typeset, designed, marketed and distributed by John N. Merrill.

© Text – John N. Merrill 1987

© Map and photographs – John N. Merrill 1987

First Published — January 1988.

ISBN 0 907496 34 2

Meticulous research has been undertaken to ensure that this publication is highly accurate at the time of going to press. The publishers, however, cannot be held responsible for alterations, errors or omissions, but they would welcome notification of such for future editions.

Set in Rockwell, medium and bold.

Printed by: Linprint, Mansfield, Nottinghamshire.

Front cover sketch — Tissington Well Dressing; Town Well.

ABOUT JOHN N. MERRILL

John combines the characteristics and strength of a mountain climber with the stamina and athletic capabilities of a marathon runner. In this respect he is unique and has to his credit a whole string of remarkable long walks. He is without question the world's leading marathon walker.

Over the last ten years he has walked more than 60,000 miles and successfully completed ten walks of at least 1,000 miles or more.

His six major walks in Great Britain are –
Hebridean Journey .... 1,003 miles
Northern Isles Journey .... 913 miles
Irish Island Journey .... 1,578 miles
Parkland Journey .... 2,043 miles
Lands End to John o'Groats .... 1,608 miles
and in 1978 he became the first person (permanent Guinness Book of Records entry) to walk the entire coastline of Britain – 6,824 miles in ten months.

In Europe he has walked across Austria – 712 miles – hiked the Tour of Mont Blanc, completed High Level Routes in the Dolomites, and the GR20 route across Corsica in training! In 1982 he walked across Europe – 2,806 miles in 107 days – crossing seven countries, the Swiss and French Alps and the complete Pyrennean chain – the hardest and longest mountain walk in Europe, with more than 600,000 feet of ascent!

In America he used the the world's longest footpath – The Appalachian Trail – 2,200 miles – as a training walk. He has walked from Mexico to Canada via the Pacific Crest Trail in record time – 118 days for 2,700 miles.

During the summer of 1984, John set off from Virginia Beach on the Atlantic coast, and walked 4,226 miles without a rest day, across the width of America to Santa Cruz and San Francisco on the Pacific Ocean. His walk is unquestionably his greatest achievement, being, in modern history, the longest, hardest crossing of the USA in the shortest time – under six months (178 days). The direct distance is 2,800 miles.

Between major walks John is out training in his own area – the Peak District National Park. As well as walking in other parts of Britain and Europe he has been trekking in the Himalayas five times. He has created more than ten challenge walks which have been used to raise more than £250,000 for charity. From his own walks he raised over £80,000. He is author of more than eighty books, most of which he publishes himself. His book sales are in excess of 2 million. His next major walk – 2,400 miles – is down the length of New Zealand.

CONTENTS

Page No.

INTRODUCTION 1

Alport Castle Woodlands Love Feast 2

Ashbourne Gingerbread 3

Ashbourne Shrovetide Football 4

Baptismal Customs 5

Barmote Court 6

Bull Baiting 7

Carnivals 9

Castleton's Garland Ceremony 10

Church Clipping 11

Cock Fighting 12

Curfew Bell 13

Derbyshire Cheese 14

Eyam Funeral Customs 15

Funeral Garlands 16

Hunts 17

Lead Mining Lore 18

Longshaw Sheepdog Trials 20

Customs relating to Love and Marriage 21

Mischief or Roguery Night 24

Morris Dancing 25

November 5th and its Customs 26

One Day Shows 27

Padley Chapel 28

Passing Bell 29

Pin Fold 30

Plague Commemoration Service 32

Riding the Stang 33

Rush Bearing 34

Shrove Tuesday and its Customs 35

Sugar Cupping 36

Tug of War 37

Well Dressing 38

Wife Selling 39

Wiffle-Waffle 40

Winster Pancake Races 40

RECIPES –

— Ashbourne Gingerbread 41

— Bakewell Pudding 42

— Buxton Pudding 43

— Derbyshire Moorland Tartlets 43

— Derbyshire Oatcakes 43

— Frumety 44

— Posset Drink 44

— Syllabub 45

— Tharf Cake 45

— Wakes Week and Cakes 46

OTHER BOOKS BY JOHN N. MERRILL 49

DERBYSHIRE

MORRIS DANCERS IN WINSTER

INTRODUCTION

The Peak District and Derbyshire area is a treasure trove of ancient customs. Many are still in practise today while others are just historical items from yesteryear. My aim of this book has been to draw together the numerous customs found in the region over the last few centuries. My interest in this side of the historical aspect derives from walking the area and seeing at first hand items such as bull rings, funeral garlands and pin folds. To learn more I began researching in the local history departments of Sheffield, Chesterfield and Derby libraries, and my thanks go to them for helping me locate many of the facts.

Customs such as Well Dressing are well known but I wanted to encompass as much variety as possible and through research learnt of many customs now ceased. Customs such as, Riding the Stang and Selling a Wife, made the research an absorbing task! As I researched I kept notes on the old customs of Love and Marraige, Roguery Night etc., so that eventually I had unearthed an interesting section. The book then is an A to Z guide of the customs, both ancient and modern, to be found in the area, and I hope it introduces many unusual facets. The Peak Park Planning Board produce the annual, Peakland Post, which apart from detailing useful information about the National Park, also has a Calendar of Events listing the dates of well dressings, wakes weeks, shows, sheepdog trials etc., held throughout the area. The Tourist Information centres also have details of "what is on". I hope this book gives you added pleasure in exploring the region and learn more about this fascinating sector of England.

HAPPY EXPLORING!

John N. Merrill

JOHN N. MERRILL
Winster, Derbyshire. October 1987.

1

ALPORT CASTLE FARM

ALPORT CASTLE WOODLANDS LOVE FEAST

Held on the first Sunday in July in a barn of Alport Castle's Farm (Grid Ref. SK135911). The term "Love Feast" is ecclesiastical, meaning a Feast of Charity, where the rich feed the poor. This annual custom is reputed to be very old, and was revived by the Methodists in the early 18th Century. John Wesley is reputed to have preached in the barn. The service commences at 11 a.m., when cake and water are handed round.

ALPORT CASTLES

The present shop has been a bakery since 1805, with the building dating back to the 15th century and formerly the Roebuck Inn.

ASHBOURNE GINGERBREAD

The origins of Ashbourne Gingerbread are lost with time. It is said to have been first made by a "baker named Porter, whose premises adjoined the lower side of the Horns Inn." The inn was situated just off the southern end of the Market Place. Today, the Ashbourne Gingerbread Shop is situated in St. John Street, and the business was established in 1887.

ASHBOURNE GINGER BREAD SHOP

3

ASHBOURNE SHROVETIDE FOOTBALL

This "royal" game of football is known to have taken place here in 1400, but its origins are unknown. The game became royal when the Prince of Wales, in 1928, set the game in motion. On Shrove Tuesday, before the game commences at 2 p.m., a lunch is held at the Green Man Hotel, where the celebrity who is to start the game has a meal with many others. The game is played by hundreds of people, and is divided into two teams. People who are born on the north side of the Henmore Brook are the Uppards, and the ones born on the south side are the Downards. The goals are two mills, Sturston and Clifton, which lie three miles apart. A goal is scored by placing the ball in the mill where the mill wheel was. At 2 p.m. the celebrity throws into the air a special ball filled with cork shavings. The two teams "play" the game, which has virtually no rules and is more of a fight to score a goal. Generally only one goal is scored, and only once has a female scored. The game continues all afternoon, and often the scene of the action is in the Henmore Brook. Usually it is darkness that calls the final whistle to the game, with neither side scoring a goal.

ASHBOURNE CHURCH

4

ASHOVER FONT

BAPTISMAL CUSTOMS

1. In Eyam, sick or diseased children were anointed with May Dew. It was strongly believed to cure. May dew was collected on May eve.

2. At Coal Aston, when a new child was brought into a house for the first time it was given an egg, some salt and a silver coin. With the silver coin a cross was made on the palm of the child's hand. If the child grabbed the coin as this was being done, it foretold a good life. There are instances when both shoes and a silver sixpence were given. This was to symbolise the wish that the child made a silvered way through a happy life.

BARMOTE COURT, WIRKSWORTH

BARMOTE COURT

Lead mining is an industry which has been carried out in Derbyshire for some 2,000 years, reaching its peak in the 1850s when over 10,000 tons were being mined. Today it is an industry of the past, and only the mine shafts and engine houses remind us of these once busy times. One custom still remains today, the Barmote Court. Following the Inquisition of Ashbourne in 1288, the Great Barmote Court of the Soke and Wapentake of Wirksworth was established that year. The Court is presided over by a Barmaster and his jury. Between them the disputes and claims are settled, and formerly the royalty from the area known as the King's Field, of which Wirksworth was the main centre, was collected. The King's Field covers an area around Wirksworth of 73,800 acres or 115 square miles. In 1852, a parliamentary Act gave the Court a legal basis.

Originally, Wirksworth dealt with the lead mines in the Low Peak and the Court at Monyash dealt with the High Peak. Other Courts were held at such places as Eyam, Stoney Middleton, Ashford and Crich. Today, Wirksworth is the only place, almost 700 years since it was first held, to hold a Barmote Court. The barmaster and jury meet in the Moot Hall, Chapel Lane. The Hall is a non-conformist chapel, and on the front wall, on either side of the entranceway, are two tablets illustrating a measuring dish and lead mining tools. The Court meets twice a year, in April and October. Formerly there were 24 jurymen who held office for six months, but today there are only 12. At the meeting the members still retain the old custom of being supplied with beer, bread and cheese, and smoke long clay pipes. Chained to the wall, but unfastened for the Court, is a brass measuring dish made in 1513 for measuring lead ore. It is believed to be the only one in the country and holds between 14 and 15 Winchester pints, about 472 cubic inches.

BULL BAITING

In almost all the villages and towns of Derbyshire from the 12th Century onwards until 1835, when it was abolished, bull baiting was one of the climaxes of the Wakes or Fairs. A bull with its horns protected was secured to a post or bull ring, usually in the centre of the village. Here the beast was harassed by dogs. Bets were laid on the dogs as to who would be able to pin the bull down by its nose. The dogs were well trained to avoid the horns and charges of the bull, but despite this many were thrown high into the air.

Several bull rings can still be seen, such as at Eyam, Foolow and Snitterton.

In the 18th Century a bye-law was passed in Chesterfield that all butchers in the Shambles who killed bulls must bait them first. If you did not, you were liable to pay a fine of 3s.4d. (16p). It was believed that baiting the bull first tenderised the meat, as well as informing everyone who sold bull beef.

Ashbourne was a popular place for bull baiting , and the animal was tied or chained to the bull ring in the market place. It is said they continued the practice long after the Act abolishing this practice became law. On rare occasions a horse has been known to be baited. Bradwell was another place where the "sport" was popular. On several occasions the bull became so maddened that he tore himself free and chased the spectators. In 1820 at Bradwell, instead of having the bull chained to a ring, the spectators formed a circle. Frank Bagshaw from Hazelbadge Hall came into the ring and shouted, "Tey him to mev; tey him to mev." As requested, he was tied to the bull's tail, and as soon as the dogs were set on the bull, the bull ran and dragged Bagshaw up Bradwell Brook!

In Tutbury, just inside Staffordshire, was the custom of Bull Running, which is said to have been started by John of Gaunt in the 14th Century. The custom was abolished in 1778. The bull was provided by the Prior of Tutbury, but later the lands belonged to the Dukes of Devonshire. The custom was a brutal one, for – "The animal's horns were sawed off, his ears cropped, his tail cut off to the stump, all his body smeared with soap and his nostrils blown full of pounded pepper." While this was being done, the steward from the Minstrel's Court proclaimed that everyone should allow the bull to pass and no-one was to get within forty feet of it, except the minstrels.

BULL RING

"A bull or bear tethered to the ring attached to a large block of stone was set upon by dogs as a spectacle for the villagers during Wakes Week . The practice was declared illegal in 1835.

The block was formerly in the centre of the Square and had been covered with successive layers of roadmaking material .

It was lifted out and removed to this site during the improvement work in the Square in 1986

EYAM BULL RING

7

The bull was let loose, and it was up to the minstrels to catch him, between the time he was released and sunset. If the bull was not caught, it became the property of the giver. However, if a minstrel managed to get hold of the bull and cut off a piece of its hair and brought it to the market cross, as proof of his deed, the bull was brought to the bailiff's house. Here a collar and rope were fastened round it before being secured to the bull ring. Then it was baited with dogs before being given to the minstrels.

As well as bull baiting at the fairs, bear baiting was equally as popular. At Ashford-in-the-Water, the bear was harassed by dogs every evening of the festivities. The bear was muzzled and secured to a ring in the centre of the village. A single dog was generally set against the bear, who was usually blind. One blow with the bear's paw often maimed the dog. The bears were not killed but were looked after by bear 'wards', who either travelled around the area or, if at a large centre of population, were kept permanently for the annual fairs. The custom was abolished, along with bull baiting, in 1835.

> "The wisdom of our ancestors
> A well known fact I'm stating,
> Thought bulls and bears, as well as hooks,
> Were suitable for baiting.
> But now this most degenerate age
> Destroys half our resources
> We've nothing but our hooks to bait,
> Unless we bait our horses."
> – Ward.

FOOLOW BULL RING

8

WINSTER: VILLAGE QUEEN c.1920

CARNIVALS

Many of the Peak District villages hold a carnival week or day, and often it is in conjunction with the Well Dressing week, such as at Tideswell, Litton and Hope. Usually there is Morris Dancing, the crowning of the Carnival Queen, processions, and a sheep roast or barbecue in the evening. Bamford, which holds their Carnival Week in mid-July, have an unusual pram race which takes place on the evening of the third Monday in July. You race in pairs, with the heaviest person in the pram, and the lightest one has to push it! The course is from the Recreation Ground to the Angler's Rest, which is most apt.

WINSTER: CARNIVAL PROCESSION c.1920

CASTLETON'S GARLAND CEREMONY

Held on Oak Apple Day, 29th May, each year, is this unique ceremony. If the 29th happens to be a Sunday, then the proceedings take place on the Saturday. There are records that state that the custom was also carried out at Bradwell and Hope, but today it is only carried out at Castleton. The custom has been celebrated in Castleton for centuries and may have been a fertility rite, but today it is said to commemorate the restoration of Charles the Second.

The garland is about three feet high and cone-shaped. It is made from wood, which is covered with straw. Onto this are tied bunches of flowers, which have been gathered the day before and on the morning of the ceremony. A small wreath of garden flowers is placed over the garland, and is known as the Queen Posy. The completed garland, which has been made on the afternoon of the 29th, weighs about 56 pounds and is ready to be lifted onto the shoulders of the King, who is dressed in Stuart costume.

The procession used to start from the Nags Head Hotel, and since 1974 from the Peak Hotel. Leading the procession is the King, who sits astride a horse with his upper body hidden by the garland. Next is the Queen, also in Stuart clothes, and this is really a youth dressed as a female. Behind is the Castleton Band, followed by the female dancers, who carry small bunches of flowers. The procession goes from the hotel to the Spital Bridge, on the northern outskirts of the village, over the Peakshole Water, before ending at the Market Place. Here the Queen's Posy is placed round the war memorial, and the garland is lifted off the King and winched to the top of the church tower, where it stays for a week. In the Market Place the girls dance the Castleton Morris Dance, and songs are also sung.

CHURCH CLIPPING

On the nearest Sunday to 8th September, Wirksworth Parish Church, dedicated to St. Mary the Virgin, is the scene of a once very popular but now rare custom, known as Clipping the Church. A procession leaves from the Market Place, and on reaching the church a hymn is sung. The party then encircle the church holding hands and sing, "We love the place, O Lord, in which Thine Honour dwells." The encirclement and holding of hands is believed to be symbolic, and to show their affection for the church. A short service is held in the church afterwards. The date when the custom first started is not known, but was revived here in 1921 and has been maintained ever since.

Another Church Clipping custom takes place at Burbage near Buxton. On the last Sunday in July, adults and children gather and a service is held. The entire congregation walk once round the church holding hands. The hymn "The Church's One Foundation" is sung. The church was dedicated in 1851, and the custom would appear to have been maintained from the 1850s to the present day.

WIRKSWORTH CHURCH

11

COCK FIGHTING

Cock fighting was one of the main attractions of fairs and wakes, as were both bull and bear baiting. In most villages of the Peak District the "sport" was avidly played, such as at Tideswell. The game was abolished in Great Britain in 1849, but is still very popular in the Arab countries today. From the time of Henry the Eighth, who had a royal cockpit built at Whitehall Palace, the game was extremely popular. Generally, the fight was between several pairs of birds, and the eventual winner was the one with the most 'victories' (deaths). It was really the survival of the fittest. There are two forms of the game; one is known as the Battle Royal, and the other the Welsh Main. In the Battle Royal, several birds were placed in the ring and left to fight amongst themselves. The winner was the one who survived whilst all his companions lay dead or dying. Naturally, before the contest began, betting took place. The birds too were well groomed and specially prepared for the battle. The Welsh Main was a more organised contest, with eight pairs starting. The eight winners from this match were paired, then the four winners, then the semi-final was held to find the overall winner. Likewise he would be the only bird left alive in the ring.

The only reference to cock fighting today is the retention of the name Cockpit in Derby; now a major roundabout near the Eagle Centre. John Speede's map of "Darbye" of 1610 shows the Cock Pit clearly. The Derby Mercury often carried advertisments for cock fighting events. The following example is taken from the Derby Mercury dated — May 6 — 13th 1784.

COCKING

A MAIN of COCKS to be fought at the houfe of Thomas Harrison, the Cock and Talbot in Tideswell, betwixt the Gentlemen of Yorkfhire, and the Gentlemen of Derbyfhire; to fhew Thirty-one Cocks on each side, for THREE GUINEAS a battle, and TWENTY the odd one: To weigh on Saturday the 15th Day of May, and fight on Monday and Tuefday following.

Feeders, J. SMITH, for Yorkfhire,

J. BRIDGET, for Derbyfhire.

TIDESWELL CHURCH

CURFEW BELL

William the Conqueror is believed to have started this custom of bell ringing, during the winter months, as a guide to travellers in the early evening on the location of their destination. The custom was abolished in 1100 A.D., but in Derbyshire the custom has been kept going for centuries, until virtually ceasing in 1939. Chapel-en-le-Frith is said to be the place where the bell has been rung longest, since 1070 A.D., but does so no longer. The Curfew Bell at Eyam was rung from 29th October to 25th March at 8 p.m.. The parents of the village used to say to their children at bedtime, "If thou doesn't get off to bed th' curfew wi' th' iron teeth will come and fetch thee." At Castleton the bell was rung from 29th September to Shrove Tuesday.

DERBYSHIRE CHEESE

Village wakes were once a special event in the village calendar. Originally a wake was the celebration of the anniversary of the founding of the church. The day was the feast day of their particular saint, to which the church was dedicated. The choir, clergy and congregation held a special service in the church, and the following day was devoted to dancing and sports. The climax of the wakes was the large meal prepared for the family and relations by the farmer's wife. Pride of place on the table was the Derbyshire cheese, a recipe that was almost lost, but is now being revived. The custom of cutting the Derbyshire cheese at the meal was a special and solemn occasion, and seems to have ceased about 1850.

The farmer's wife made a special cheese each year for this meal. She lavished extreme care over the cheese, making sure it was kept in the right room with the right temperature. The cheese was covered with calico, but the edges were turned over exposing the cheese, in two bands about one and a half inches wide. As the weeks passed, these bands turned a pale green colour as mould began to form. The protected part remained an amber colour. From the colour the farmer's wife could work out what the cheese was like and when it was ready for eating at its best. On the feast day, the cheese was brought in with due celebration and placed in the centre of the table. It was the master of the household who held the right to cut the cheese. Generally a quarter was cut out first to be sampled by all. This was the moment of truth, for as everyone tasted it the farmer's wife would know whether her careful work had been worth it.

CHEESE PRESS, KELSTEDGE NR ASHOVER

14

CHEESE PRESSES, HARTINGTON

EYAM FUNERAL CUSTOMS

1. It was considered unlucky for a man to be buried without tears being shed for him.

2. An unmarried girl had a garland made of white satin ribbons and carried in front of her coffin, at the funeral procession. The garland was placed in two green sticks of willow and carried by four white-clad girls.

3. Before the funeral procession could begin, the mourners were given triangular-shaped cakes, which they carried in a handkerchief to the church. The cakes were usually spiced, and had currants in. The mourners also drank a dark liquid known as "burnt drink". This was an ale spiced with cloves, nutmeg, ginger and mace. The mourners would stand at the door of the house and consume the liquid before the procession began. As the mourners walked beside the coffin, they sang continuously. The tankard and the willow basket that the cakes were handed round in were kept for all funerals.

4. Before the burial service, the coffin was watched all night, and the custom was known as "lich-waking". A candle stood at either end of the coffin.

FUNERAL GARLAND

FUNERAL GARLANDS

Miss Anne Seward, the Lichfield poetess, wrote about Eyam in 1790 –

"Now the low beams with paper garlands hung,
In memory of some village youth or maid,
Draw the soft tear from thrilled remembrance sprung;
How oft my childhood marked that tribute paid.
The gloves suspended by the garland's side,
White as its snowy flowers with ribband tied:
Dear village! Long may these wreaths funereal spread
Simple memories of the early dead."

The custom of making funeral garlands for the funeral procession of young unmarried females was extremely popular in the 17th and 18th Centuries. The custom seems to have completely died out in about 1820, and was reserved for females who were betrothed but died before their planned marriage. Upon her death a garland was made. Its shape was similar to a birdcage and was made from thin strips of wood. Around this were wrapped white ribbons, and at the joins were hung rosettes. Hanging down from the centre would be a paper glove or handkerchief, and upon this would be recorded the name, age and date of the person concerned. At the funeral procession a young woman from the village would carry the garland in front of the coffin. After the proceedings the garland would be hung in the church above the deceased's person's pew.

Glover, in his "History and Gazetteer of the County of Derby", writes –

16

"When unmarried women were buried their companions carried
"garlands" made of wreaths of flowers – emblems of youth
and purity. Garlands were hung up in the church in a
conspicuous place in memory of the deceased. Hathersage
and Glossop were noted places. At the latter place a
garland of ribbons and artificial flowers etc. is said to
have cost 30p."

Other places which are known to have had garlands in the past include Alvaston,
Ashford-in-the-Water, Ashover, Bolsover, Eyam, Fairfield, Glossop, Hathersage,
Heanor, Hope, Matlock, Tissington, Trusley, West Hallam and South Wingfield.
Today there are only three places in Derbyshire where they can be seen.
Ashford-in-the-Water has four, St. Giles' Church in Matlock has five in a glass
case, and Trusley in South Derbyshire has one in a glass case.

The ones in Ashford still hang from the beams, but the writing on the gloves is
now illegible. One said – "April 12th 1747, Ann Howard, aged 21."

Another said –

"Be always ready, no time delay,
I in my youth was called away:
Great grief to those that's left behind,
But I hope I'm a great joy to find."

Ann Swindel, aged 22 years, December 9th 1798.

"To her sweet memory flow'ry garlands strung,
On her now empty seat aloft were hung."

HUNTS

Three hunts operate during the hunting season – November to April – in
Derbyshire. The Meynell and South Staffordshire Foxhound Hunt covers the
South Derbyshire and South Staffordshire area. Prior to 1970 these areas were
covered by two separate hunts – The Meynell Hunt and South Staffordshire Hunt
– but they amalgamated in May of that year. They meet on a Tuesday, Thursday
and Saturday. Operating in the northern uplands of the county is the High Peak
Hunt with a pack of harriers. These dogs are smaller than a foxhound, and are
basically used to hunt hares – in this case long-legged mountain hares. They hunt
twice a week during the season on Wednesday and Saturday. The High Peak
Hunt also organise the annual Point to Point Races held on Easter Tuesday on
Flagg Moor. There are usually six races, with the first commencing at 2 p.m..

Hunting the area to the east of the River Derwent and the north-eastern side of
the county is the Barlow Foxhounds Hunt. They are unique to the county, being
privately owned, and are one of the few in Britain to be so. A pack of foxhounds
has between 20 and 60 couples of hounds. The Master of the Hunt who trains
them also controls them in the field. The Huntsman looks after the hounds in the
kennels and is responsible for bringing them to the meet. Whippers-in help in
the kennel and in bringing them to the meet. They also encourage trailing dogs.

BARMOTE COURT, WIRKSWORTH — PLAQUE

LEAD MINING LORE

Lead mining, being such a major industry of the Peakland scene in previous centuries, has evolved its own lore and numerous customs. Published in 1653 was a poem of 300 lines written by Edward Manlove, the Steward of the Wirksworth Barmote Court. These lines, which the miners learnt by heart, detail the old customs. The book was titled, "The Rhymed Chronicle of Edward Manlove, concerning the liberties and customs of the lead miners within the Wapentake of Wirksworth, Derbyshire."

> "By custom old in Wirksworth Wapentake,
> If any of this nation find a rake,
> Or sign, or leading to the same he may set
> In any ground, and there lead ore may get.
> They may make crosses, holes and set their stowes,
> Sink shafts, build lodges, cottages, and coes,
> But churches, houses, gardens, all are free
> From this strange custom of the minery."

If a death in a mine –

> "If perchance a miner damped be,
> Or in the mine be slain by chance medley,
> The Bergmaster or else his deputie,
> Must view the corpse before it buried be.
> And take inquest by jury who shall try
> By what mischance the miner there did die."

If found guilty of stealing lead for the third time –

> "Shall have a knife struck through his hand to the haft
> Into the stow, and there till death shall stand,
> Or loose himself by cutting loose his hand;
> And shall forswear the franchise of the mine,
> And always lose his freedom from that time."

18

Miscellaneous Lead Mining Lore –

1. An 18th Century writer described Derbyshire lead miners as being –
   "Lean as a skeleton, pale as a corpse, his hair and beard
   a deep black, his flesh dark, and, as we thought,
   something of the colour of the lead itself."

2. Regarding Castleton lead miners –
   "They ate seven meals a day, had good teeth, and
   were fond of oats!"

3. On no account were you allowed to whistle in a mine, for to do so would frighten away the ore!

4. Miners in Bradwell would not work underground on Good Friday, but would work above if requested. On Christmas Eve, they left a candle burning in the mine for the "Old Man".

5. Women were rarely ever allowed down a lead mine. The miners believed that if they were this would lead to disaster.

6. Many of the old lead miners referred to "Knockers". Upon enquiry as to who they were, they replied – "About 18″ high and rarely seen, but heard; seem to work in the mines."

BARMOTE COURT, WIRKSWORTH — PLAQUE

FOX HOUSE INN

LONGSHAW SHEEPDOG TRIALS

Held at the beginning of September each year on three consecutive days – Thursday, Friday and Saturday – and a major event in the Derbyshire calendar. In 1896 a group of shepherds met in the Fox House Inn and planned to have a pigeon shoot. The date was fixed for 24th March, 1898, to take place on Totley Moors. However, the idea was soon abandoned, as most of the shepherds knew very little about the sport and few had guns anyway. It was suggested, therefore, that they hold a dog trial instead, and this was agreed. March 24th turned out to be bad weatherwise, with a severe snowstorm blowing. It was decided to hold the trials the following day on Timothy Field, which lies below the main entrance to the Longshaw estate and on the right-hand side of the Grindleford road. The trials were a success, and the only prize was a Scotch sheep. From 1898 the trials have been held annually, and take place on the opposite side of the road in the large field in front of Longshaw Lodge.

LONGSHAW LODGE

DERBYSHIRE CUSTOMS RELATING TO LOVE AND MARRIAGE

1. At midnight on St. Valentine's Eve, an unmarried girl should, as the clock strikes twelve, run round the church several times and repeat –
   "I sow hempseed, hempseed I sow;
   He that loves me best
   Come and after me now."
Her lover and husband-to-be will appear before her.

An instance of this occurred in Ashbourne in 1820. The young woman ran round the church twelve times. So intent was she in her task that by the time she had finished she was totally exhausted. She fainted and had to be carried home, where she later died!

2. On St. Valentine's Day, unmarried girls should look through the keyhole of the hen house. If they see a cock and hen together, they know that they will be married before the year ends.

3. Before a bride leaves the house, boiling water is poured over the doorstep. The reason being that before it dries another wedding will be arranged in the house. Another custom states that the boiling water is poured on to the step after the bride and groom have entered the house. The next girl to cross the water, provided her dress becomes wet, will be the next to marry.

4. It is considered to be very unlucky to be married during May.

5. A Derbyshire woman on her wedding day should wear –
   "Something old, something new,
   Something borrowed, something blue."

6. When to get married?
   Monday for health
   Tuesday for wealth
   Wednesday the best day of all
   Thursday loses
   Friday crosses
   Saturday no luck at all

7. On St. Mark's Eve, 24th April, sit in the barn and your future wife will walk through the door. It is recorded that one person did this, and, instead of his wife walking in, a spade and pick came in. He knew he would never marry.

8. If a male abandons his lover, she should get a piece of his hair and boil it. As the water boils, her lover will not be at peace.

9. On All Hallows Eve, unmarried females place a crooked sixpence and a sprig of rosemary under their pillows. As they sleep they will dream of their future husbands.

10. At Curbar, a young man was unfaithful to his lover. She took a live frog and stuck numerous pins into it before burying it. Having done so, her lover is said to have suffered from pains in all his limbs. In due course he came back to her and apologised. She dug up the frog and removed the pins, and on doing so her lover's pains deserted him. They married soon after.

11. If a woman's lover will not come or shuns her affection, the woman on going to bed carries a shoulder of lamb. As she walks up the stairs she must say –
"It's not this bone I wish to stick,
But my true lover's heart I mean to prick;
Wishing him neither rest nor sleep
Until he comes to me to speak."
On reaching the bedroom door, she should push a penknife into the shoulder blade.

12. At both Eyam and Coal Aston the following custom is known to have been carried out. If a young man had abandoned his mistress and married another, on the morning after the ceremony a garland was hung from a tree near his mistress's home. The large garland was made from flowers, evergreens, dragon lilies and ribbon. This was suspended from the tree, together with an onion and a bottle of urine.

13. Courting girls from another village presented problems in the olden days. The males of Bradwell who did so had to pay a fine known as "Cock-walk" or "Foot-ale" to the males of the village from which the girl came from. At Bradwell the fine was 1s.6d. (7½p.) and in other villages it was 1/- (5p). Provided you paid the fine you were left alone, but, if you did not, the villagers would put a halter around your neck and parade you through the streets. The fine was equally divided amongst the young men, who generally spent it on ale.

14. One day of the year was known as "Lousing" or "Unlousing" Day. This was the day when the men could lift up a girl and kiss her. It is known to have taken place in Wormhill, Baslow, Bamford, Hathersage and Bradwell. A young man in Hathersage did this on the day in question, and was fined for his action. In Bradwell, if a man meets a woman while outside, he is quite in order to "unlouse" her – to steal a kiss. Easter Monday was Unlousing Day in Castleton.

15. A well in Bretton is known as the Dewric Well. A woman who drinks from the water is said to be made fruitful.

16. On St. Valentine's Day, the boys of Castleton are allowed to kiss the girls. At one time, the schoolmaster there disagreed with the custom and sent the girls home early!

17. It is said that if a couple of lovers consent to marriage under the shadow of Peveril Castle, the vows should never be broken. If they are, their future love affairs will never come to anything.

18. On St. Valentine's Day in the 19th Century there was a custom of "Sweeping the Girl", for –
"If the lass is not kissed or does not get a visit from
her sweetheart on St. Valentine's Day, she is said to
be dusty, and the villagers sweep her with a broom, or
a wisp of straw. She is bound, subsequently, to cast

lots with other girls, and, finally, if she has good
luck, draws the name of her future husband out of an
old top hat."

19. To help bring about a marriage, the female should stand in front of the mirror. In one hand she should hold a candle, and with the other she must eat an apple and comb her hair, simultaneously. As she is doing this, her husband-to-be should appear.

20. A female wishing to find out who her husband-to-be is should eat a raw herring for supper. All of it should be consumed, including the bones. That night, the woman will dream of her lover.

21. To learn of her future husband, the female should stick a row of pins into her sleeve while singing the Lord's Prayer. Within twenty-four hours she will see her future husband.

22. On a certain day (I don't know which one), if a girl fasts and only drinks pure water, her handsome lover-to-be will appear.

23. To dream of her future husband, the female should go to a friend's house. Before going to bed she should knit her left garter around her right stocking. During the night she will dream of her future husband, who will salute her with a kiss.

24. In Bradwell, until about 1880, was the following wedding custom. Before anyone could get married they had to pay a toll. Where the bride and groom were to pass on their way to the church, a rope was stretched across the road. Alternatively, the church gates were locked. Only when the groom had paid the toll charge was the obstacle removed. The "toll-keepers", on receiving the money, hurried over to the nearest pub!

25. In Eyam and Stoney Middleton, they carried out a custom known as "clay-daubing". After the young couple were married, the guests together built a mud house, which they completed before they left. After building it, they generally enjoyed much drink and food.

26. Following a wedding in Stoney Middleton, a rope was fastened across the road along which the newly married couple would pass. On reaching the rope the villagers would throw sods of earth, old shoes and rice at them. After this the rope was removed, and they were allowed to continue their journey. It was believed that sods denoted luck in their produce grown from the ground, the shoes meant they would have plenty of clothes, and rice meant plenty of children.

MISCHIEF NIGHT

Although either termed the Mischief or Roguery Night, and held at different times of the year in different villages, the general misdemeanours are the same. The custom was popular in the 19th Century. The boys of the village, after dark, would pull the gates off the hinges and put them in a tree, remove a cart and place it in a brook, or throw bricks down your chimney. However, by placing a brush, shovel or broom outside your door, the mischievous boys would miss your household. In Bradwell, Mischief Night was Christmas Eve. In Great Longstone, this was the eve of Shrove Tuesday. Here all the items the boys collected were placed in a circle around the village cross. The villagers in the morning had to go and collect their belongings. At Tideswell everything was hidden, and the owners had to search for their gate or cart.

GREAT LONGSTONE

MORRIS DANCERS AT HARTINGTON

WINSTER MORRIS DANCE TEAM c.1952

MORRIS DANCING

Throughout the Peak District during the summer months, at many of the villages such as Bakewell, Castleton, Eyam and Tideswell, Morris Dancers will be seen. The origin of the dancing is not know, although it is likened to fairy dances. In its present form it dates back to the 15th Century, and is named after the Spanish word, Morisca, which means a Moorish play or dance. Several of the Peak District villages have their own special Morris Dance, such as at Tideswell, where it is known as the Tideswell Processional Morris. One of the major places to see the dancers is at Winster during their Wakes Week, which is held at the end of June or early July. They have four dances of their own, known as the Morris Dance (Winster version), the Winster Gallup, the Blue-eyed Stranger and the Winster Reel. To add to the fun of the proceedings, they have a Fool, King and Queen. The Queen is always a youth dressed as a woman, and the parts of both the King and Queen can be played by anyone, as they are not required to dance!

NOVEMBER 5TH AND ITS CUSTOMS

1. Most villages celebrated the day with a huge bonfire in the market square. The village who had been doing it the longest was Chapel-en-le-Frith, but this ceased in 1935. On that day they would gather a huge pile of material around the Cross. Naturally this did not do the stone cross much good when it was set alight.

2. The children of Tideswell on 5th November went around the village begging for wood and chanting the following:-
   "Coal, Coal, a bonfire hole,
   A stock and a stake,
   For King George's sake.
   If you please will you give me a penny
   For my bonfire hole."

3. Many people used to make Thar Cakes on 5th November. Usually they are made from oatmeal, a little flour, a pinch of salt and plenty of treacle. The end product is a sweet, sticky cake which was handed around the family in the evening. This was known as Thar Cake Joining, and the cake was extremely popular with the children.

CHAPEL EN LE FRITH CROSS

ONE DAY SHOWS

Bakewell Show was formerly a one-day Show – the largest in the country – and dates back to 1848. Now it is held on a Wednesday and Thursday in early August each year. More than 40,000 people attend to visit the many manufacturing stalls; to see the floral displays; cattle judging; and show-jumping competitions. Major attractions such as sky diving or the Household Cavalry highlight the afternoon's events.

The village of Hope holds an annual agricultural Show and sheepdog trials on late Summer Bank Holiday Monday.

Also in August, horticultural shows are held at Edale, Litton, Grindleford and Froggatt.

PADLEY CHAPEL

Situated near Grindleford Station, this historic building is of more than usual interest. The Manor House dates from the 14th Century, but is now lost and only the outline of the buildings can be seen today. The Chapel, which was originally the gatehouse to the Manor, is the only building intact, and has a 14th Century hammer beam roof. Two of the principal owners of the Manor House were Roman Catholic families, the Eyres and the Fitzherberts. The latter were the owners in the 16th Century, when the most important period of the Manor's history took place. The Fitzherbert family were, like other Roman Catholics, persecuted by the Protestants. Sir Thomas Fitzherbert would not renounce his faith and was, therefore, sent to prison. He died thirty years later in the Tower of London in 1591.

On 12th July, 1588, two Roman Catholic priests, Nicholas Garlick and Robert Ludlum, were arrested here. Twelve days later they were hung, drawn and quartered in Derby. After this the Manor House was little used and slowly fell into decay. The Chapel weathered the time, and by the 1890s it was being used as a hay store and cow byre. In 1933 Monsignor Paine of Derby purchased the Chapel and restored it. The colourful stained glass windows record the Chapel's past history. Held on the nearest Thursday to 12th July is an annual pilgrimage from Grindleford Station to the Chapel, in memory of the two Padley martyrs. A similar pilgrimage is held in September.

**THE ARREST AT PADLEY CHAPEL AND EXECUTION AT DERBY —
WINDOWS IN PADLEY CHAPEL**

PADLEY CHAPEL

PASSING BELL

Many Derbyshire churches rang the Passing Bell –
- 3 tolls for a girl under 16
- 4 tolls for a boy under 16
- 5 tolls for a woman
- 7 tolls for a man

was the usual table. The people of Chapel-en-le-Frith believed that the passing bell was rung while the dying person was still alive. This was so that his friends knew of his or her imminent death, and they could pray for their friend before life was extinguished. At Eyam they believed that if the sound of the passing bell was clear, another death in the village could be expected.

CHAPEL EN LE FRITH CHURCH

PIN FOLD

Many Derbyshire villages still have their "pin folds", which are walled enclosures where stray cattle were placed. A "Pinner" was appointed, and he had the authority to impound any stray cattle he found. The only way of getting your cattle back was by paying an agreed price per head. Pin folds can be seen at Hathersage and Tideswell. The one in Tideswell was made in 1787 as cattle were straying onto the churchyard. The charge per head was fixed at 1/- (5p). A story is told in Tideswell that, juat before the annual wakes, a certain man would release his wife's cattle. The pinner, as arranged, would impound them, and would only release them again when she had paid the charge. The pinner and her husband split the money between them, as agreed, so that they could have a good time at the Wakes! Mr. Joseph Dale, who died in 1943, was the last pinner of Tideswell. He also held another village post, that of town crier.

TIDESWELL PINFOLD

HATHERSAGE PINFOLD

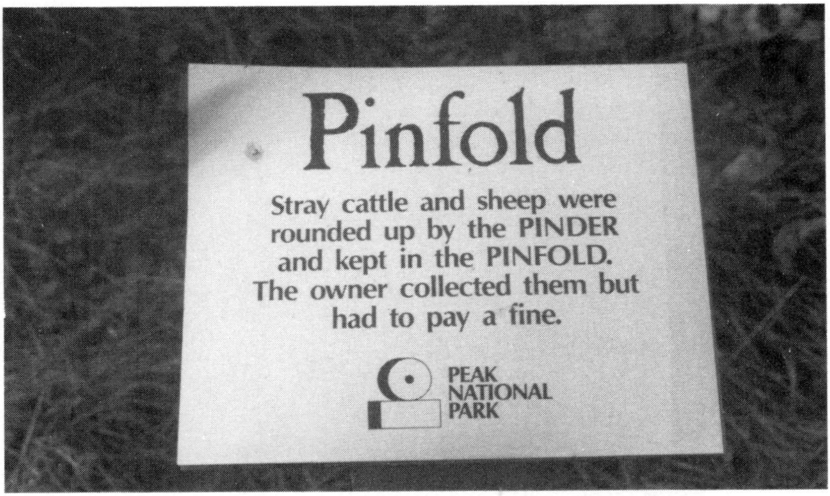
Pinfold
Stray cattle and sheep were rounded up by the PINDER and kept in the PINFOLD. The owner collected them but had to pay a fine.
PEAK NATIONAL PARK

Clearly marked on John Speede's "Darbye" map of 1610 can be seen the fenced Derby Pinfold, but nothing remains today. In Curbar at the bottom of Pinfold Hill at G.R. SK250746 is a magnificent circular high walled pinfold.

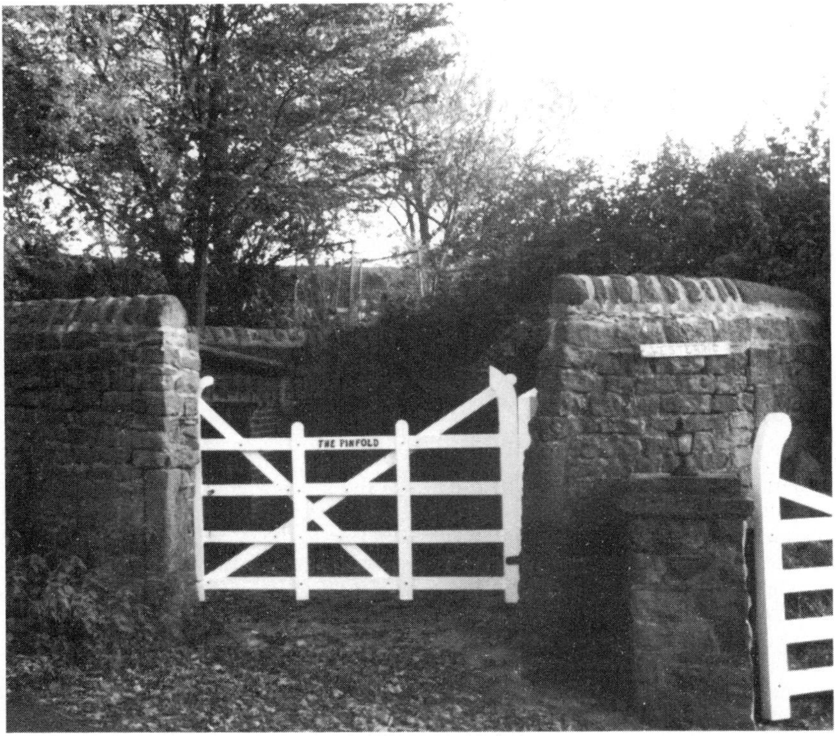
THE PINFOLD

CURBAR PINFOLD

MOMPESSON'S WELL ABOVE EYAM

EYAM PLAGUE COMMEMORATIVE SERVICE

A commemorative service to the victims of the Eyam Plague is held on the last Sunday in August each year. Out of 350 villagers, 267 died from the bubonic plague which ravaged the village in 1665-66. Due to the strong personality of the Rector, William Mompesson, the disease was contained within the village and did not spread to the surrounding area. During the plague, to prevent the disease spreading, the daily church services were held outside on a grassy mound known as the Cucklet Delf. Since 1905 an open-air service has been held here in memory of the plague victims. In 1965, on the 300th anniversary of the plague, the then Archbishop of York, Dr. D. Coggan, was the preacher. A procession leaves Eyam Parish Church at 2.30 p.m., and the service at the Delf commences at 3.00 p.m..

RIDING THE STANG

This old custom, which ceased at the end of the last century, was generally widespread throughout Derbyshire and was often referred to as Ran Tanning. If a married couple rowed frequently and either the man or the woman beat the other, this custom was carried out. For three successive days, usually Tuesday, Wednesday and Thursday, a large group of people would walk through the village or town. They would create a large noise by beating on tins and shouting away. They would carry shoulder-high a man, who was renowned for his wit and humour. Often he would be paraded on a donkey or carried in a cart, as in Coal Aston, near Dronfield, in 1880. Every few yards the parade would stop and be silent while the man would recite a poem about the deeds of the couple. The opening lines would be something like this:-

> "Ran, Tan, Tan – Ran, Tan, Tan,
> ...... has beaten her good man."
> or ...... has beaten his woman."

The wit would then go into more details of what had been happening, an example of which is as follows:-

> "Here we come with a ran, dan, dong;
> It's not for you, nor for me, we ride this stang;
> But for Gooseberry Bob, whose wife he did bang.
> He banged her, he banged her, he banged her indeed;
> He banged her, poor creature, before she stood need.
> He took up neither tipstaff nor stower,
> But with his fist he knocked her backwards ower;
> He kicked her, he punched her, till he made her cry,
> And to finish all, he gave her a black eye.
> Now, all you good people that live in this row,
> We would have you take warning, for this is our law:
> If any of you, your wives do bang,
> We're sure, we're sure, to ride you the stang."

If the beating was known to be excessive, the parade often carried an image of the beater, made from straw. On the last night they would burn this in front of the offender's house. A case of this is recorded to have taken place in Coal Aston in 1880, when the wife's friends gathered together to publicise the husband's wrong doing. They also believed that by carrying the image round three nights in succession, the man cannot "have the law" on you. Other cases occurred in Ashford-in-the-Water.

A similar custom also took place in Coal Aston in 1888. A man and a woman were engaged to be married, and on the Saturday before the wedding was scheduled to take place they bought the ring. The wedding was to have taken place on the Monday, but in the intervening period they had a row and the ceremony was called off. On the Monday evening the boys of the village made straw images of the man and woman, and these were burned opposite their respective houses. The idea was that the burning of the image caused either pain, or death, to the person it represented.

RUSH BEARING

Before church floors were either boarded or stone-flagged, the earth floor was covered with rushes once a year. The custom was very popular in the 17th and 18th Centuries, but from the early 1800s the custom decreased, until it ceased by the end of that century. The Forest Chapel, near Macclesfield, is the only place in the Peak District where the ceremony takes place today. Among the many places where the custom was carried out are Chapel-en-le-Frith, Glossop, Peak Forest, Whitwell and Ashover. Generally the rush bearing ceremony was held at the end of August, but there were exceptions, for both Peak Forest and Whitwell held theirs on Midsummer's Eve.

Rushes were cut from somewhere in the parish. At Chapel-en-le-Frith this was done on Rushup Edge, near Mam Tor, as well as from a field nearby known as Poors Piece. At Ashover, heather and bracken were also used, and at Whitwell, in east Derbyshire, hay was cut from a field known as Church Close. Once the rushes were cut, they were loaded into carts which were decorated with ribbons and flowers. On the day of the ceremony these were pulled through the village or town with much gaiety. In front of the parade danced Morris dancers. At the church the cart was unloaded, with everyone lending a hand to carry the rushes into the church, where they were spread out on the floor, filling the church with a beautiful smell.

Parish Registers of these times record the expenses of the ceremony, and these are an example:-

1758 Given to Morris Dancers at Rushbearing – 3s.0d. (15p)
1792 Spent at Rushbearing – £1.8s.4d. (£1.42p)
1803 Expenses of a rush cart – £2.2s.0d. (£2.10p)

"Behold the rush-cart and the throng
Of lads and lasses pass along!
Now watch the nimble Morris dancers,
Those blithe, fantastick, antic prancers,
Of ribbons in a gay confusion
Of brilliant colours, richest dyes."
By Elijah Ridings, from " Village Festival".

FOREST CHAPEL, NR MACCLESFIELD

SHROVE TUESDAY AND ITS CUSTOMS

1. The day before Shrove Tuesday was known as Collop Monday. The poorer people of Derbyshire visited their richer neighbours and begged for a collop of bacon. This was used on Shrove Tuesday as fat for the frying pan, when making the pancakes.

2. At Abney, the boys of the village on Shrove Tuesday would be up very early. The one who was last out of bed was known as a "bed-churl" or "bed-churn". He was usually thrown into the ash midden. At Eyam they had a similar custom, and here the boys would be up at 2.00 a.m.. They would walk round the village rattling tins, blowing on cow horns and generally creating a din. The boy who was last out of bed was known as "the bed churn" for the rest of the day.

3. At Whaley Bridge, on Shrove Tuesday, the young females of the household had to be capable of eating a pancake between the time one had been made and the next. If they had not consumed one in that time they were thrown into the nearest gooseberry bush or ash midden.

4. At Dronfield Grammar School, a special bell known as the "Pancake Bell" was rung in the morning for half an hour. Once it had stopped ringing, everyone was allowed home for the rest of the day. Many of the children would make their way to church, where they would walk around with large baskets, for it was believed that pancakes were thrown over the steeple on that day.

5. Many villages had a "pancake bell", which was rung at 11.00 a.m. as a reminder to the womenfolk to mix their batter.

6. At Winster on Shrove Tuesday, each year, are held Pancake Races. You race between the Dower House and the Market House. As you run, you should continually toss your pancake in the frying pan. Naturally, if you drop the pancake you must stop and pick it up before continuing. When the custom started is unknown, but it has definitely been recorded since 1870.

WINSTER PANCAKE RACES — CHILDRENS

SINNERS WELL UNDERNEATH GREAT SHACKLOW WOOD

DOR WELL, DROPPING TOR, TIDESWELL

SUGAR CUPPING

In the 18th and 19th Centuries on Easter Sunday morning, many of the Derbyshire villagers drank sugar and water at a nearby well. The custom, which to them was religious duty, was their means of expressing joy and happiness at the resurrection of Christ. The villagers of Ashford-in-the-Water went to "Sinners Well" underneath Great Shacklow Wood. The people of Tideswell went to "Dropping Tor".

TUG OF WAR

At many of the Wakes Weeks or Carnivals held during the summer months, one of the features on the agenda is a Tug of War contest. In the 19th Century it was a very popular sport, and a major inter-village competition. This century the sport declined, but more recently it has mushroomed out and new clubs are being formed. Derbyshire is no exception, and has a thriving number of clubs. All are registered with the Tug of War Association.

A contest is between two teams, and the best of three pulls decides the winner. The maximum number to a team is eight men. The total weight of the team is known so that the team fits into one of the weight grades, and is equally paired to another team of the same weight. This ensures that the contest is not just one of strength, but of skill and quick reactions. The rope is between 4 and 5 inches in circumference, and more than 35 yards long when a full team is pulling. The winning pull is when the centre mark on the rope passes over one of the outside marks. Both indoor and outdoor competitions are held.

TISSINGTON WELL DRESSING

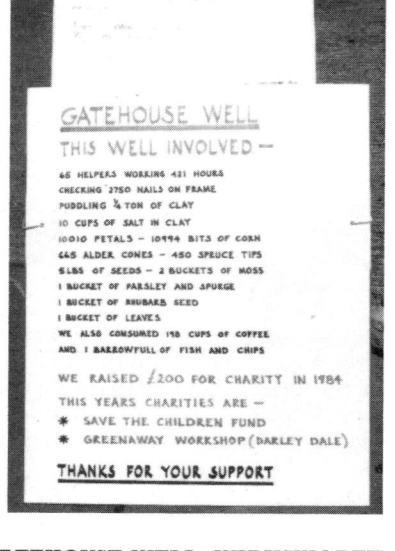

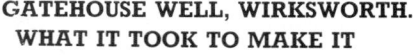

GATEHOUSE WELL, WIRKSWORTH.

WELL DRESSING AT WIRKSWORTH   **WHAT IT TOOK TO MAKE IT**

WELL DRESSING

In a large proportion of the limestone villages of the Peak District, this unique and special Derbyshire custom is carried out. It is generally agreed that the custom dates back to 1350. During the Black Death of 1348-49, nearly all the Derbyshire priests died. Tissington was one place that remained uncontaminated, and it is said that this was because of the pure water of their five wells. As an offering to their good fortune, they dressed the wells with flowers as a form of thanks. Although the custom has often lapsed for periods since then, the custom was revived in 1950 and has become extremely popular, with many more villages reviving the custom. Tissington is first every year, on Ascension Day. The wells remain dressed for a week, as they do in the other villages. Following Tissington, there is a well-dressing ceremony almost every week until early September.

Beside each well is a mosaic of flowers, generally depicting a biblical scene, church or major event. These mosaics of flowers are the work of the village, and are renowned for their accuracy, depth of feeling and colourful array. The flower petals are pressed onto a clay base. Numerous types of flowers are used, together with moss, bark, corn, etc., to create a picture which never fails to arrest one's attention. Usually on the Saturday afternoon, the wells are blessed, and for the next week remain on show to the public. Very often at the end of the week is a Carnival or Sheep Roast, as at Eyam and Ashford-in-the-Water. Villages where the custom takes place are Ashford-in-the-Water, Barlow, Belper, Bonsall, Bakewell, Bradwell, Buxton, Cutthorpe, Dore, Eyam, Hope, Litton, Marsh Lane in Eckington, Matlock, Pilsley, Stoney Middleton, Tideswell, Tissington, Wirksworth, Wormhill, Wyaston and Youlgreave.

SELLING A WIFE

WIFE SELLING

In 1808, Brand wrote —

    "A remarkable superstition still prevails among the
lowest and of our vulgar, that a man may lawfully
sell his wife to another, provided he deliver her
over with a halter about her neck. It is painful
to observe that instances of this occur frequently
in our newspapers."

Until the first Divorce Court in 1857, the only way to divorce your wife was by special Act of Parliament, which cost approximately £3,000; equivalent to about £28,000 today. To get round this, among the poorer people they had a wife-selling custom. On Market Day you brought your wife to the market with a halter around her neck. You paid the necessary toll, which gave you the right to sell your goods. You then paraded her about the market square, telling everyone of her good points. Having stirred up sufficient interest, you then auctioned her off to the highest bidder. Papers were drawn, and the sale was completed in a nearby pub. The landlord often hired a town cryer for an hour to inform everyone of the sale. This brought him a great deal of business, as many people came to see the new couple.

Although there are many instances of sales in the Midland counties, and especially in Paradise Square in Sheffield, where the sale was done over a few glasses of ale, I can find only one reference to a sale in Derbyshire. I am convinced there were many more.

On 5th December 1772, Thomas Bott sold his wife to a man from Langley Common for 18d. (9 pence) in Derby market place. This was quite an average price. There is an example in Stafford, where Cupid Hudson sold his wife for 5s.6d. (28 pence) in 1800. The highest price I have found so far is 25/- (£1.25p), but this was not for a Derbyshire woman!

WIFFLE-WAFFLE

In the olden days when a field of hay was cut by hand, the scythe blade was sharpened by hand. The sound of sharpening the blade sounds like the word "wiffle-waffle". A tale is told about it, for the devil lost a mowing match with a Derbyshire farmer. They each had a large area to cut, and the loser of the contest was the person who had to sharpen his scythe first. Unknown to the Devil, the farmer had placed iron sticks into the ground of the Devil's area, so that when he started cutting he had to sharpen first.

WINSTER PANCAKE RACES

Shrove Tuesday has always been a special day on the customs calendar. Being the day before the beginning of Lent, it was usual in olden times to make your confession, or "shriving" as it was called. The word shriving explains the naming of the day, Shrove Tuesday. The day was also an excuse for feasting, to eat up any food that could not be eaten during Lent or would not be palatable after Lent.

The origin of the annual Pancake Races at Winster is not known. Nor is the date when they first commenced, but they have been a feature of the village calendar for well over 100 years. Winster is the only Derbyshire village to uphold this custom. The main street is closed to traffic while the races take place. The course is approximately 100 yards long, from the Dower House to the Market House. They commence at 3 p.m., and the age of the contestants decides the yardage of the race. The six-year-olds start from about 20 yards from the Market Place, and the men from the gates of the Dower House. The races follow strict rules. Special small frying pans are used. The pancakes are made to a special recipe so that they are robust and will not disintegrate from the rough punishment, and can be stood upon without bursting. Naturally, they are not designed for eating but for the rudiments of the race! As you run you must toss the pancake three times. The first three home in each group receive a small prize.

**WINSTER PANCAKE RACE
PARTICIPANT**

RECIPES

ASHBOURNE GINGERBREAD

8 oz. butter
10 oz. plain flour
2 level teaspoons of Jamaica ginger
5 oz. caster sugar
Pinch of salt
Grated lemon rind, or finely chopped candied peel

Cream together butter and sugar until quite soft. Sift in flour, ginger and salt, and add peel. Knead with the hands until a smooth dough is obtained. Roll out with the hands into a long roll about 1″ thick, cut into lengths 2″ long. Put on lightly greased baking tray and bake for about 20 minutes in moderate oven at 350°F.

BAKEWELL PUDDING SHOP

41

BAKEWELL PUDDING

Bakewell has become synonymous with the much loved, delicious puddings made and originating from there. The town's name, sadly, does not have its origins in the puddings. In the 10th Century it was named Badecan Wiellin, meaning 'Badeca's stream'. The recipe for the pudding was created by accident. During the latter half of last century, in about 1859, Mrs. Greaves, the mistress of the Rutland Arms, Bakewell, gave instructions to her cook for a strawberry tart, as she was expecting important visitors for lunch. She instructed her cook to make the pastry, spread egg mixture onto it and strawberry jam on top. Somehow the instructions were misunderstood, and the jam was put in first with the egg mixture on top. After the meal, the visitors complimented Mrs. Greaves, who was the sister-in-law of Sir Joseph Paxton, on the excellent pudding. When they had departed, Mrs. Greaves went to see her cook and learned of the mistake. Instead of being reprimanded, the cook was instructed to continue making the puddings that way, as they have been ever since. The recipe was left to a Mr. Radford in Mrs. Greaves' Will. Upon his death it passed to a Mr. Bloomer, whose son still makes the puddings to this original recipe.

BAKEWELL PUDDING
Ingredients:-
Yolks of 5 eggs
6 oz. caster sugar
Almond essence
Whites of 3 eggs
4 oz. butter
Strawberry jam
Method:-
Line flan ring or baking tin, traditionally oval, about 7" across, with puff pastry, spread with strawberry jam, and cover with egg mixture made as follows:-
Melt together butter and sugar, and mix in the egg yolks and whites and almond essence. Bake in hot oven, Regulo 7 or 425°F. for a quarter of an hour, then in medium oven, Regulo 4 or 350°F. for 25 minutes.

BAKEWELL PUDDING
This recipe is very old, and is stated to have been used to make the Bakewell puddings served to the late King Edward and Queen Alexandra when they visited Chatsworth years ago.

Ingredients:-
A quarter pound butter
2 eggs (yolks only)
A quarter pound sugar
Almond flavouring to taste
Method:-
Cream the butter and sugar, add egg yolks and beat thoroughly. Put into a jar in a pan of water and let boil until as thick as cream. When nearly cold add flavouring. Line some saucers with a rich pastry spread with a layer of raspberry jam and cover with mixture. Bake in a quick oven till lightly brown on top.

BUXTON PUDDING

The weight of two eggs in breadcrumbs, sugar and butter. Beat the butter to a cream, add the other ingredients, including the eggs, well-beaten. Line the sides of a dish with pastry, put a layer of jam at the bottom and pour the mixture over. Bake in a moderate oven.

DERBYSHIRE MOORLAND TARTLETS

Ingredients:-
2 eggs, boiled hard and finely chopped
3 oz. butter or marg.
A quarter pound sugar
A quarter pound chopped candied peel
A quarter pound currants
A little grated nutmeg

Warm butter, then add the other ingredients to form a spread. Line patty tins with pastry and fill with mixture. Bake until set.

DERBYSHIRE OATCAKES

Ingredients:-
Half a pound of fine or medium oatmeal
Half a pound of plain flour
Half an ounce of yeast
Salt
1 teaspoon sugar
Warm water

Method:-
Sift oatmeal, flour and salt into a warm bowl. Cream yeast and sugar together, add half a pint of warm water and pour into dry ingredients, mixing gradually until a thin batter is formed; extra warm water may be needed. Allow to stand in a warm place until well risen, about 20 minutes. Have ready a heated girdle or electric hot plate heated to a moderate oven, grease with beef or pork fat. Pour on a small cup of batter and cook until batter is set and lightly browned on underside, then turn and bake other side. Should be eaten hot, fried in bacon fat or toasted.

FRUMETY

At the end of sheep-shearing, or sometimes at the conclusion of the corn harvest, Frumety was drunk. The custom was considered to be a form of thanks-offering for the work completed. Frumety was made from wheat boiled in milk, which was sweetened and spices such as cinnamon and nutmeg were added. Everyone brought their own spoon and basin. The custom was once widespread, but it seems that from about the 1850s it ceased altogether.

POSSET DRINK

Until about the 1880s it was a very popular custom on Christmas Eve for the young people to drink posset. Nearly every household in the 18th Century owned a posset-pot, which was generally large and shaped like an urn. The posset drink was made from milk, ale, eggs, currants and spices, and was considered a most delicious drink. Even teetotallers would forget their principles at this time to drink the liquid. Generally about half a dozen people gathered round the urn and were allowed to take one ladleful only of the liquid. Just prior to this, a ring and a silver coin were slipped into the drink. Apart from being a good drink in its own right, the main attraction of the custom was to procure either the coin or ring in the ladle. The one who fished the ring out could be certain to be married soon, and definitely within the next twelve months. The marriage would also be a happy one. The one who secured the coin could expect to have a year of good luck and to be successful in money matters.

ALMOND POSSET

"To make an Almost Possett" – taken from a recipe book published in 1814:-

"Grate the crumbs of a penny loaf very fine, pour a pint of boiling milk upon them, and let them stand two or three hours; then beat it exceeding well; add to it four ounces of almonds blanched, and beat as fine as possible, with rose water; and a quart of good cream; mix them all well together, and set them over a slow fire; boil them a quarter of an hour; then set it to cool, and beat the yolks of four eggs, and mix with your cream; when it is cold, sweeten it to your taste; then stir it over a slow fire till it grows pretty thick, but do not let it boil, or it will curdle; then put it in a china bowl and send it up with a few macaroons to swim on the top. It is proper for a top dish at supper."

SYLLABUB

This Derbyshire custom, now long since abandoned, is similar to posset drinking. The drink was made by pouring wine into a bowl, which was then sweetened with sugar. A cow was then milked straight into the wine so that the drink was frothy. The drink was then poured into wine glasses. A ring and silver coin were placed into two of the glasses. When the guests were about to leave, everyone helped themselves to a glass. The unmarried were extremely anxious in selecting a glass, for upon this depended their marital state. The one with the ring knew he or she would be the next to marry. The one who had the silver coin would die unmarried.

To make Syllabubs – Both recipes taken from a recipe book published in 1814.

"Take a pint of cream and a gill of new milk, a few lumps of sugar rubbed on the rind of a lemon; take a chocolate mill and froth it; take off your froth and lay it on a hair sieve; keep taking off your froth as long as it rises; half fill your glasses with white, and have the same number of glasses half filled with red wine; put into each glass a little sugar, and lay on your froth as high as you can. If you have any orange-flower water by you, put a little in and it will give them a nice flavour."

To make a Syllabub under the cow:-
"Put a bottle of strong beer and a pint of cyder into a punch bowl, grate in a small nutmeg, sweeten it to your taste, then milk as much milk from the cow as will make it a strong froth and the ale clear; let it stand an hour, then strew over it a quantity of currants, and send it to the table."

THARF CAKE

To make a Tharf Cake – taken from a recipe book published in 1814:-

"Take a quarter of a stone of treacle, a pound of lard or butter, melt your lard and treacle together; take three pounds of oatmeal, a quarter of a pound of carraway seeds, half a pound of raw sugar, a little lemon peel cut fine, and a teacupful of brandy; mix it up with your treacle and butter, make it up into cakes, lay them upon tins, and bake them, but not too hard."

THOR CAKES

– Eaten on 5th November and peculiar to Wirksworth.

Ingredients:-
1 lb. fine oatmeal
1 lb. flour
Three quarters of a pound of butter
1 lb. sugar
2 oz. candied peel
1 lb. treacle
2 teaspoons baking powder
1 teaspoon coriander seeds
1 teaspoon ground ginger
1 teaspoon salt

Method:-
Rub butter into dry ingredients and add warmed treacle. Knead a little and roll fairly thinly. Cut into rather large rounds and bake in a moderate oven.

WAKES WEEK

"The return of the wake never fails to produce a week, at least,
of idleness, intoxication, and riot."
The Claybook Historian, 1791.

Looking at the summer events programme for the Peak District, you will see that several villages hold Wakes Weeks, such as Hope and Winster. Today, the events such as tug-of-war competitions and Morris dancing are held in the evenings. Originally the wake was a solemn occasion to celebrate the feast day of the saint to whom the village church was dedicated. The feast day is taken as the day of the death or burial of the saint. Originally a night of prayer was celebrated in the church, but later this was abandoned and the feast day became a village holiday, with feasting and drinking. In the 18th Century it was a whole week of revelry, and special wakes cakes were made for the occasion. Some of these recipes survive, and are given below. Today, the wakes week is largely a thing of the past, and only a few uphold what was once the highlight of the village calendar.

WAKES CAKE RECIPES

ASHBOURNE

Ingredients:-
2 cups of butter
2 cups of sugar
1 egg
4 teaspoons of ground ginger
4 cups of self-raising flour
Half a cup of citron, shredded
A few currants

Method:-
Cream butter, sugar and ginger. Add beaten egg and mix well. Add finely shredded citron and flour and mix all together to make a firm dough. Roll out very thinly on floured board. Cut into rounds. Press in a few currants. Bake in moderate oven (375oF.), dropping temperature to 350oF. until cakes are crisp and lightly browned.

LANGLEY

Ingredients:-
1 lb. of flour
Half a pound of butter
6 oz. of sugar
A quarter pound of currants
Half an ounce of carraway seeds
Half a teaspoon of ground ginger
Half a teaspoon of baking powder
Essence of lemon

Method:-
Warm half the butter, mix all other things, then oiled butter. Knead well together, roll out and cut into small cakes. Bake in a moderate oven.

MELBOURNE

Ingredients:-
One and three quarter pounds of plain flour
1 lb. of butter
Half a pound of caster sugar
A little cream
A quarter pound of currants
2 eggs
2 teaspoons of baking powder

Method:-
Rub butter into flour, add sugar and currants, then mix with eggs and cream. Roll out thinly like biscuits and bake in a moderate oven until lightly brown. When cold, store in tin and, before use, scatter icing sugar on rather thickly.

WINSTER

Ingredients:-
Half a pound of plain flour
6 oz. butter
6 oz. caster sugar
1 egg
1 oz. of currants

Method:-
Rub flour and butter together, add sugar and currants, mix to a stiff dough with beaten egg, knead a little, roll out and bake in a moderate oven. The cakes should be a pale golden brown and the size of a saucer.

WIRKSWORTH

Ingredients:-
One and a half pounds of flour
1 lb. of butter
1 lb. of sugar
Pinch of salt
A few currants
Carraway seeds
1 teaspoon of carbonate of ammonia
2 tablespoons of cream

Method:-
Beat these to a cream, adding 1 teaspoonful of carbonate of ammonia at the last. Stir in flour, a few currants and carraway seeds and two tablespoonsful of cream. Roll out thinly and cut into rounds. Bake in a moderate oven to a pale brown.

OTHER BOOKS BY JOHN N. MERRILL PUBLISHED BY JNM PUBLICATIONS

DAY WALK GUIDES –

SHORT CIRCULAR WALKS IN THE PEAK DISTRICT
LONG CIRCULAR WALKS IN THE PEAK DISTRICT
CIRCULAR WALKS IN WESTERN PEAKLAND
SHORT CIRCULAR WALKS IN THE STAFFORDSHIRE MOORLANDS
PEAK DISTRICT TOWN WALKS
SHORT CIRCULAR WALKS AROUND MATLOCK
SHORT CIRCULAR WALKS IN THE DUKERIES
SHORT CIRCULAR WALKS IN SOUTH YORKSHIRE
SHORT CIRCULAR WALKS AROUND DERBY
SHORT CIRCULAR WALKS AROUND BUXTON
SHORT CIRCULAR WALKS AROUND NOTTINGHAMSHIRE
SHORT CIRCULAR WALKS ON THE NORTHERN MOORS
40 SHORT CIRCULAR PEAK DISTRICT WALKS
SHORT CIRCULAR WALKS IN THE HOPE VALLEY

INSTRUCTION & RECORD –

HIKE TO BE FIT....STROLLING WITH JOHN
THE JOHN MERRILL WALK RECORD BOOK

CANAL WALK GUIDES –

VOL ONE – DERBYSHIRE AND NOTTINGHAMSHIRE
VOL TWO – CHESHIRE AND STAFFORDSHIRE
VOL THREE – STAFFORDSHIRE
VOL FOUR – THE CHESHIRE RING

DAY CHALLENGE WALKS –

JOHN MERRILL'S PEAK DISTRICT CHALLENGE WALK
JOHN MERRILL'S YORKSHIRE DALES CHALLENGE WALK
JOHN MERRILL'S NORTH YORKSHIRE MOORS CHALLENGE WALK
PEAK DISTRICT END TO END WALKS
THE LITTLE JOHN CHALLENGE WALK
JOHN MERRILL'S LAKELAND CHALLENGE WALK
JOHN MERRILL'S STAFFORDSHIRE MOORLAND CHALLENGE WALK
JOHN MERRILL'S DARK PEAK CHALLENGE WALK

MULTIPLE DAY WALKS –

THE RIVERS' WAY
PEAK DISTRICT HIGH LEVEL ROUTE

PEAK DISTRICT MARATHONS
THE LIMEY WAY
THE PEAKLAND WAY

COAST WALKS –

ISLE OF WIGHT COAST WALK
PEMBROKESHIRE COAST PATH
THE CLEVELAND WAY

HISTORICAL GUIDES –

DERBYSHIRE INNS
HALLS AND CASTLES OF THE PEAK DISTRICT & DERBYSHIRE
TOURING THE PEAK DISTRICT AND DERBYSHIRE BY CAR
DERBYSHIRE FOLKLORE
LOST INDUSTRIES OF DERBYSHIRE
PUNISHMENT IN DERBYSHIRE
CUSTOMS OF THE PEAK DISTRICT AND DERBYSHIRE
WINSTER – A VISITOR'S GUIDE
ARKWRIGHT OF CROMFORD
TALES FROM THE MINES by GEOFFREY CARR

JOHN'S MARATHON WALKS –

TURN RIGHT AT LAND'S END
WITH MUSTARD ON MY BACK
TURN RIGHT AT DEATH VALLEY
EMERALD COAST WALK

COLOUR GUIDES –

THE PEAK DISTRICT.....Something to remember her by.

SKETCH BOOKS – by John Creber

NORTH STAFFORDSHIRE SKETCHBOOK

CUSTOMS OF THE PEAK DISTRICT & DERBYSHIRE BY JOHN N. MERRILL

THE AUTHOR RE-INACTING WIFE SELLING IN EYAM

The Peak District is world renowned for its unique and colourful well dressing custom. This book descibes this and many other customs in practise today in the area. Many lesser known ones and others that have ceased are also detailed making this a handy A to Z historical guide to the ancient and modern customs of the area.

a J.N.M. PUBLICATION

ISBN 0-907496-34-2

9 780907 496342

£2.75